World Religions General Editor: Raymond F. Trudgian
Principal Lecturer and Head of the Religious Studies
Department, Borough Road College, Isleworth, Middlesex

UNDERSTANDING YOUR JEWISH NEIGHBOUR

MYER DOMNITZ

*Secretary and Education Officer of the
Central Jewish Lecture Committee of the
Board of Deputies of British Jews*

2226926

296

LUTTERWORTH EDUCATIONAL
GUILDFORD AND LONDON

First published 1974

ISBN **0 7188 1801 6**

Copyright © 1974 Myer Domnitz

Printed in Great Britain by
Cox & Wyman Ltd., London, Fakenham and Reading

CONTENTS

LIST OF ILLUSTRATIONS

For permission to reproduce the above photographs, the Author and Publishers are indebted to: The Board of Deputies (for numbers 1 and 14), The Jewish Museum (for numbers 2, 3, 5, 10, 11, 13, 16, 17, and 18), Israel Embassy (for numbers 4, 6, 9, and 14), Israel Tourist Office (for numbers 7, 8, and 19) and Youth Aliyah (for number 15).

All biblical quotations are taken from: The Holy Scriptures, New Translation: Jewish Publication Society of America.

If you would like further information about the Jewish people or suggestions for activities, at home or in school, you can write to the author: Myer Domnitz who is the Secretary and Education Officer, of the Central Jewish Lecture Committee of the Board of Deputies of British Jews, Woburn House, Upper Woburn Place, London, WC1H 0EP.

EDITOR'S INTRODUCTION

The response to our *Thinking About* series showed the need for basic foundation books which could be used by pupils in Junior and Middle Schools. The books in this *Understanding Your Neighbour* series presents the festivals, places of worship and other customs of the various faiths now represented in this country.

The children who use these books will have reached what Jean Piaget, the educational psychologist, calls the 'concrete' stage of thinking. This is defined in *Religious Education in Primary Schools* (Schools Council Working Paper 44) as the stage where, 'the child now begins to be able to think more logically, to relate different aspects of a situation, to classify data, and to check over his thinking. He is still limited, however, to thinking mainly about specific objects . . .'

This research has been born in mind in the preparation of these books. It is now becoming accepted that World Religions can be dealt with at the Junior and Middle School level by introducing the specific festivals and customs of other people. Another accepted approach is through the use of themes such as 'light' and 'water', elements known to the pupil which recur practices of many religions.

The General Article introducing the Christian Education Movement Primary Resource material on 'Living in a Multi-Faith Society' agrees that this phenomenological approach is the way to study other faiths in the classroom but states that this method 'Can easily degenerate into a "bits and pieces" method'. It goes on to say:

> Most religious beliefs and practices can be understood only in the context of the faith as a whole, and great care must be taken therefore to select only those examples which are not misleading when studied apart from that context . . . While pupils cannot be expected to see religion as a whole, teachers should not venture into the field of other faiths without the support of good resource material and without the willingness to study the religion seriously and gain some sort of overall understanding.

We have attempted to present this 'overall' picture in these books in such a way that not only the teacher but also the pupil can come to a balanced understanding of their neighbours' faith.

The specific and concrete examples of events, customs and buildings are presented in the context of the faith in order to help the pupil not only to acquire new facts but to perceive the experience of a child who lives in another culture.

Through the study of this series of books pupils should be able to discover their own themes and to see the similarities and differences.

Again to quote from the CEM Primary Resource material,

> World Religions in Education is certainly not an attempt to gloss over differences, to pretend that all religions are really the same, but it does help pupils to see that the religious quest is common to mankind, that certain elements are found in most religions, e.g., worship, sacred places, sacred writings, beliefs about the significance of man, a sense of the mystery of life, etc. even the form may vary. The emphasis is on what unites men rather on what divides them.

This is the emphasis of these books as they seek to lay a foundation of knowledge and appreciation in the Primary school to counteract the stereotype so prevalent in their environment which often prevents them from 'Understanding their Neighbour'.

Isleworth, Middlesex   Raymond F. Trudgian

AUTHOR'S INTRODUCTION

This short book on Judaism, which describes Jewish festivals, and some practices, institutions and ideas, is for children aged nine to thirteen; it is intended to give them some understanding of an ancient faith of which Christianity and Islam are daughter religions. Judaism is practised by modern Jews in many parts of the world.

The material in the book is based on the information provided in response to thousands of requests which I have received from children, young people, and adults over many years, as the Secretary and Education Officer of the Central Jewish Lecture Committee of the Board of Deputies.

I thank Miss Carolyn Scott for her editorial assistance and helpful suggestions.

London, 1973   M.D.

Note: All Hebrew words are given their English meanings.

7

THE STORY BEGINS

This story is about a voyage of discovery made by a Jewish boy called David Cohen, when he was twelve years old. It was one year before his Bar-mitzvah: his religious coming of age.

Ever since he was five, David had attended a Jewish religion school on Sunday mornings and after school during the week. His family had brought him up to observe Jewish customs and practices from the day he was born.

Already David had begun to realize that although he belonged to a people and a faith with a very long history, it was also a people and a faith very closely linked with the world today.

At school, David's friends often asked him about his religion, and so with two other Jewish boys, Jack Levy and Jonathan Samuels, he decided to explore Judaism and find out more of what lies behind its traditions and ceremonies and the colourful stories surrounding them.

The obvious place to begin the exploration seemed to be with their own names.

1. At School.

DAVID

(1 Samuel 16–31; 2 Samuel; 1 Kings 1–2; 1 Chronicles 11–29)

David, the shepherd boy who became king, was probably one of the most exciting characters in the whole Bible. Anointed by the prophet Samuel to follow Saul as king, he was thought of as the founder of the biblical state of Israel.

David, the youngest of the eight sons of Jesse, was called from looking after his father's sheep near Bethlehem, to play his harp to soothe Saul when he was very depressed.

When Goliath, the Philistine giant, challenged a man from Saul's army to fight him, David said to Saul: 'Your servant will go and fight this Philistine'. Saul made David put on a brass helmet, a coat of mail, and a heavy sword. But David put these aside and instead he took five stones from a brook and his sling. When Goliath mocked David because he was so young and unarmed; he replied 'You come to me with a sword, a spear and a javelin, but I come in the name of the Lord', and he killed the giant with a stone from his sling.

He captured the fortress of Zion, a desolate, rocky place in the kingdom of the Jebusites which became the City of David. Today the City of David is called Jerusalem.

And David loved God. One day he danced before the Lord with all his might because the Ark of the Covenant containing the Tablets of the Ten Commandments was being brought into his city, Jerusalem.

David was a hero; a great man and a great king. But the Hebrew Bible never hides anything, and it does not hide the faults of even the greatest human characters. David, for all his greatness, had his weaknesses too, and when the prophet reproached him for his sins, he repented and was forgiven.

King David left behind him songs, psalms which people love to read because they tell of human experiences: joy and gladness, sorrow, sickness, defeat and triumph, success and failure. Of the 150 psalms, 73 are headed 'Le David . . .' meaning a song of (or for) David, and they are used every day as readings or Hebrew prayers.

But perhaps best of all, young David and his schoolfriends loved the tradition about King David that has been told and retold over the generations.

A harp hung above King David's couch, and when the midnight breeze touched the strings of the harp, it made such striking music that David who was a great musician, felt the urge to wake up and spend the hours till dawn rose in the eastern sky, writing religious poetry and holy words.

The psalms of David, says the tradition, contain the stirring music of man's heart, swept by God's hand.

But that was all past, and some of young David's friends were impatient with the past. They were interested in what King David's story had to tell them today.

Young David learned something from his famous namesake which was very important for the present. He learned that for all his faults, King David was a great man. He also learned that David was descended from the faithful Ruth, and Ruth was to be the ancestress of the Messiah, the servant of God, who was one day to establish a perfect kingdom of peace, justice and compassion.

It was a wonderful day to look forward to, when all human beings would be linked together as God's children. But it seemed to young David that he and his friends had a great deal of preparing to do, a great deal of improvement to make in their daily conduct and behaviour, before they could hope to be blessed with the coming of that wonderful time.

COHEN

David knew that his surname, Cohen, meant priest. The name was linked with Aaron, the great grandson of Levi (Levy), a son of Jacob. Aaron, the elder brother of Moses, was the first High Priest. From him were descended all the succeeding High Priests of Israel, and the Hebrew priests, the Cohanim.

In the time of the temple, thousands of priests used to take turns serving there. They wore white linen robes and had many duties including the offerings in the tabernacle and temple.

The High Priest, in addition to his ordinary functions as a priest, was the

11

only one allowed to enter the Holy of Holies on the Day of Atonement, the holiest day in the Jewish calendar, to atone — to offer sacrifice and ask forgiveness — for himself and all the people.

The High Priest, as well as his white robes, had wonderful vestments, and David read about them in Exodus 28 and 29:1–7. He wore blue robes with golden bells, a gold breastplate with the names of the twelve tribes in diamonds, and an embroidered vestment covering his front and back. On his head he wore a cap or turban of linen, with a golden band placed around his forehead inscribed with the words 'Holiness to God'.

The priests used to bless the people every day from the platform of the temple. In Israel, the blessing is still chanted each morning. In the synagogue David attended, it was chanted on the festivals, although in some synagogues it is chanted every Sabbath as well. David looked forward to the time when he would join the other Cohanim (of priestly descent) in blessing the people.

They are the words which the Lord gave to Moses so many years ago as a blessing for his people. The Cohanim, descendants of the priests, cover their heads and hands with their praying shawls, raise their hands towards the congregation, and chant:

> The Lord bless thee, and keep thee;
> The Lord make his face to shine upon thee, and be gracious unto thee;
> The Lord lift up his countenance upon thee and give thee Peace.
> (Numbers 6:24–26).

JACOB LEVY

Jack's name came from the Jewish name Jacob. Jacob, with Abraham and Isaac, was one of the Patriarchs (the fathers) of the Jewish people, and the boys read all about his exciting travels in the ancient lands of the Near East from Genesis, the first book of the Hebrew Bible.

They read about Jacob's wonderful dream (Genesis 28:10–17) when he saw angels climbing up and down a ladder to heaven, and the Lord standing at the top of the ladder saying: 'I am the Lord God of Abraham, thy father, and the God of Isaac: The land whereon thou liest, to thee will I give it, and to thy seed . . . and *behold I am with thee, and will keep thee in all places whither thou goest.'*

And they read that when Jacob woke up he said 'Surely the Lord is in this place and I knew it not!' Which was a thought which excited the boys very much.

They became so interested in his story that they read on; and later in Genesis (32:25–31) they read that Jacob struggled all night with an angel. With the light breaking, he made the angel bless him, with the new name of Israel, to become the name of his children and their children's children and of the whole land of Israel.

One of Jacob's twelve sons was called Levi — just like Jack's surname, Levy. And that name, Levi, became the name of one of the twelve tribes of Israel. The Levites assisted priests in the tabernacle on temple days, and they looked after the temple buildings, they were choristers and instrumentalists, playing the harps and the flutes and the cymbals which were used in singing psalms and worshipping God.

Jack often thought about the original Levites, who recited their psalms every day in the temple: 'May the Lord bless thee out of Zion; Mayest thou see the good of Jerusalem all the days of thy life — peace be on Israel.'

JONATHAN SAMUELS

Reading about his famous namesake, Jonathan, in the Hebrew Bible, made Jonathan realize what it *really meant to be friends with someone*. It made him look on David and Jack and his other friends in quite a different way, even though he wasn't sure it meant that he was ready to die for them. Because that was what Jonathan in the Bible was prepared to do for David his friend.

He and David were like brothers, and their friendship lasted even when he knew that David would become the next king, although Jonathan was King Saul's son. When he knew that his father, in a fit of madness, was going to try and kill David, he risked his life to warn his friend, and when Saul and Jonathan died in battle, David tore his clothes and wept and said:

'O Jonathan, I am distressed for thee. My brother Jonathan: Thy love for me was wonderful.'

To learn about his surname, Samuels, Jonathan read the whole of the two books of Samuel in the Bible.

He read about Samuel as a little boy, brought up in the temple by the wise old priest, Eli, and he read about God calling Samuel in the night, and Samuel's answer: 'Speak, Lord, for thy servant heareth.'

He read how Samuel grew up to become a judge, settling the people's quarrels, a priest and teacher, telling them about God and teaching them the law of Moses, and a prophet, training others to go out and share their faith with everyone they met, singing and dancing and praising God.

It was exciting when all three boys had traced the origins of their names, because Jonathan found that Samuel was commanded by God to 'hearken to the voice' of the people and 'make them a king' — The king was Saul. And Samuel supported Saul until he sinned and broke God's commands, and then Samuel anointed David as King of Israel in his place.

In the end, all the stories Jack and David and Jonathan had been reading were linked up.

A NEW BABY

David was the youngest member of his family. He had a father and mother, a sixteen-year-old brother called Joshua, and two sisters, Sarah who was twenty and eighteen-year-old Esther. He also had a cousin called Miriam, and there was great rejoicing because Miriam had given birth to her first baby — a boy. The boys went to visit her and see the new baby, and prayers were offered by those present for the well-being of them both.

On the eighth day from the baby boy's birth, there was a ceremony in Miriam's home, called the circumcision or initiation into the Covenant that God made with Abraham, these are the words about it in the Hebrew Bible:

> I am God Almighty; walk before me and be thou whole-hearted . . . and I will establish my covenant between me and thee and thy seed after thee throughout their generations for an everlasting covenant, to be a God unto thee and to thy seed after thee. (Genesis 17:1–7.)

After the ceremony, the boy was named Isaiah. Everyone said prayers for Isaiah, as: 'Even as this child has entered into the Covenant, so may he enter into the Torah,' (Hebrew for teachings of Judaism), 'the marriage canopy, and into good deeds.'

14

NAMING OF A FEMALE CHILD

The boys were in the synagogue a week later, on the Sabbath, when a member of the congregation, the father of a baby girl, was called to the public reading from the Sefer Torah (scrolls of the first five books of the Hebrew Bible). The mother was also present. The minister blessed the parents and uttered a special prayer for the welfare of the mother and the little girl. He announced the name of the baby girl — Rebecca.

REDEMPTION OF THE FIRST-BORN SON

As a Cohen, David found it very interesting to attend the service for the redemption of the new baby Isaiah on the thirty-first day from his birth. As the first-born son he was sanctified to God's service, mentioned in the Hebrew Bible (Exodus 13:2), but was redeemed when the father presented baby Isaiah to the Cohen and said 'This (is) my first born and the Holy One, blessed be he, has given command to redeem him.' (Number 18:16.) The Cohen received the redemption money, the silver equivalent of five shekels which David knew was a biblical coin. This is given to charity. The happy occasion was attended by many friends and relatives and was followed by a party in Miriam's home.

A HOUSE IS DEDICATED

Soon after Miriam's baby was born, some friends of David's parents moved into a new house, and all David's family went to the consecration of the new home. There were beautiful words from Psalm 15: 'Lord, who shall abide in your tent? Who shall dwell in thy holy mountain? He that walks blamelessly and works righteousness and speaks truth in his heart!' And chanting too: 'I will walk within my house in the integrity of my heart, I will set no base thing before mine eyes' (Psalm 101).

In Hebrew, the word for blessing is 'Berachah'. Four sections were recited from the long Psalm 119, and David's father pointed out to him that the initial letters made up the word 'Berachah'. Again, the words were very beautiful:

> With my whole heart have I sought Thee — Blessed art Thou O Lord . . . teach me Thy statutes — I do not forget Thy Law . . . The beginning of Thy word is truth — all Thy commandments are faithfulness . . . Make me to tread the path of Thy commandments; for therein I delight.

Then they said a prayer:

> Grant that members of the household may dwell together — in brotherhood and fellowship — and may meditate in Thy Law and be faithful to its precepts . . . Bestow Thy blessing upon the master of this house . . . and upon their sons and daughters the spirit of wisdom and understanding.

MEZUZAH AND OTHER VISIBLE REMINDERS OF GOD

On the right-hand door-post of the new home, there was a little case, exactly the same as the little case on the door-post of David's house, and the houses of Jack and Jonathan. After the ceremony, some of David's schoolfriends wanted to know what the case was.

David did his best to explain to them.

The case was called the mezuzah, 'a reminder of God's presence', and Jewish families always have a mezuzah, because in the book of Deuteronomy (6:4–9 and 11:13–21) there is a divine ruling which says: 'And thou shalt write them upon the door-post of thy house and upon thy gates.'

The small case is fixed on to the right-hand post of the front door, and of each inside door of a Jewish home. Inside it are the first two paragraphs of the celebrated Hebrew prayer, the 'Shema' beginning with the words:

16

2. Mezuzah.

Hear O Israel, the Lord our God, the Lord is one — and thou shalt love the Lord thy God with all thy heart and with all thy soul and with all thy might . . . (Deuteronomy 6).

and also words from Deuteronomy 11:13–21, which contains the divine ruling.

The other children were so interested that Jack went on to explain more of the outward signs which Jews display to show their devotion to God.

He told them about the tephillin, which David would wear after his Bar-mitzvah, containing four hand-written biblical passages and put on by adult Jews during weekday morning prayers in fulfilment of the command to bind the words of God 'for a sign upon thy hand and as frontlets between thine eyes'. The tephillin are known as phylacteries which in Greek is 'a means of protection'. The Hebrew word tephillah, explained Jack, which means *prayer*, is a more exact meaning. The wearing of the tephillin, like the mezuzah on the door-post, was another outward sign of devotion.

Then Jonathan pointed out to another visible reminder of God: the fringes on the tallith or praying shawl, as the Lord said to Moses:

Speak unto the children of Israel, and bid them that they make them . . . fringes in the borders of their garments . . . and it shall be unto you for a fringe, that ye may look upon it, and remember all the commandments of the Lord, and do them; (Numbers 15:37–39).

THE SABBATH AT HOME

In the home and in the synagogue, light plays a very important part. Every Sabbath Eve, David listened as his mother said a prayer before kindling the candles. The prayer included the words:

Lord of the Universe, I am about to perform the sacred duty of kindling the lights in honour of the Sabbath — grant that peace, light, and joy ever abide in our home. For with Thee is the fountain of life: in Thy light do we see light.

The candles were lit in the dining-room. After lighting them, his mother covered her eyes with her hands and said the blessing: 'Blessed art Thou, O Lord, King of the Universe, who sanctified us by Thy com-

3. Kiddush Goblets.

mandments and commandest us to kindle the Sabbath lights.'

David, Jack and Jonathan went to the synagogue, together on the Sabbath eve. The service they went to was called 'the welcoming of the Sabbath'. When David arrived home, his father blessed all his children, placing his hands over their heads. To his sons, David and Joshua, he said: 'God make thee as Ephraim and Manasseh,' the sons of the great Joseph. To his daughters, he said: 'God make thee as Sarah, Rebecca, Rachel and Leah,' the wives of the Patriarchs of the Jewish people. Then he gave the famous blessing of the priests, which David heard so often in the synagogue:

> The Lord bless and keep thee.
> The Lord make his face to shine upon thee; and be gracious unto thee,
> The Lord lift up his countenance upon thee and give thee Peace.

19

After the Blessing, he read slowly from the Book of Proverbs some well-known verses which are a tribute to Jewish wives and mothers:

A woman of valour who can find? For her price is far above rubies. The heart of her husband doth safely trust in her . . . she openeth her mouth with wisdom; and the law of kindness is on her tongue . . . her children rise up and call her blessed . . . (Proverbs 31:10–31.)

The Sabbath meal had been prepared carefully by David's mother and sisters, and the meal, like so much else, was a reminder of wonderful things that had happened in the past.

The well-baked loaves, called by the Hebrew word Challoth, placed before David's father, were covered with a cloth with religious designs embroidered on it. The loaves were a reminder that God sent miraculous food called manna for the Israelites to eat when they wandered for forty years in the wilderness. On the sixth day of each week, God sent a double portion of manna, like the two pieces of bread before David's father, so that no work should be done by Jews on the Sabbath.

David's father recited Kiddush over a glass of wine. Kiddush meant the proclaiming of the holiness of the Sabbath: a reminder that God blessed the seventh day and made it holy, thus a reminder of the creation of the world and the departure of the Jewish slaves from Egypt.

The wine was made from grapes ripened in the Holy Land, and David's father blessed it with these words: 'Blessed art Thou O Lord, our God, King of the Universe, who creates the fruit of the vine.'

When the family had drunk the wine, a blessing was said over the bread: 'Blessed art Thou, O Lord our God, King of the Universe, who brings forth bread from the earth.'

The Sabbath meal was a festive, happy occasion. David's father told a story about a Roman Emperor who asked a Rabbi, a great Jewish teacher, why the Sabbath dishes had such a fragrant smell. The Rabbi said it was because a special spice called the Sabbath was used.

'Please give me some of it,' the Emperor begged, and the Rabbi replied that the spice was only effective when people kept the Sabbath as a day of delight in God's name.

They sang happy songs called 'Zemiroth', Sabbath table songs. Then when they had finished eating, the Grace was recited — prayers showing that God provides food for his children because of his loving-kindness, his goodness and his mercy, and that there is no need for gifts from other people, because God will give all that is necessary.

20

David went with Jack and Jonathan to the Sabbath Morning Service in the synagogue and they enjoyed the Sabbath meal on their return.

On the Sabbath afternoon, David went to visit some friends, and then on to the afternoon and evening services at the synagogue.

At the end of the Sabbath, he came home from the synagogue with his father and Joshua, and his father said a special prayer called Havdalah, also said in the synagogue to mark the separation of the Sabbath from the weekdays. He made a blessing over a glass of wine, and David handed him him a spice box, and he blessed that too and passed it round to all the family so that they could inhale its fragrance. This was to show that they hoped the fragrance of the Sabbath would linger on through the whole of the following week.

His father said a blessing over the lighted candles, a reminder that on the first day, God created light. Jewish families thus bless the light on the eve of the beginning of each new week.

RE-LIVING THE PASSOVER

The Festival of the Passover was a great event in the lives of David and his family, as it is for all Jews. David always looked forward to it. It was very exciting to relive the experiences of the early Jewish people, who had been slaves for over four hundred years in ancient Egypt; to hear how they were delivered from slavery by God, how they wandered for forty years in the wilderness, eventually learning how to become *a free people again*, able to worship God away from the pagan cults of Egypt.

The night before the Passover, David, Jack and Jonathan all joined their fathers searching for leavened bread in every room of their homes. David's mother and sisters had already removed every trace of leaven they could find, because of the biblical rule: 'You shall put away leaven out of your houses' during the eight days of Passover (Exodus 12:15). David carried a little wooden basin, and when he found a few crumbs, he swept them into the basin with a feather.

The next morning, the crumbs were burned with any leaven left over from breakfast, and the special Festival crockery was brought out.

On Passover Eve, the whole family went to the synagogue for the first evening service of Passover. Then a party of friends and relations came home with them to celebrate the first night of the Passover.

21

David's mother had put a beautifully embroidered cloth on the table, with a lighted silver candelabrum which made the design look even more beautiful. On the first two nights of Passover, there was the historic Seder or ancient religious home service.

Everyone read from one of the oldest books in Judaism called the Haggadah. Haggadah is Hebrew for 'telling', and is taken from a verse about Passover: 'And thou shalt *tell* thy son in that day, saying "It is because of that which the Lord did for me when I came forth out of Egypt."' (Exodus 13:8.)

The service started with David's father reciting the Kiddush over the wine. Four goblets of wine were drunk during the service. David's father told him that one reason for drinking four goblets of wine was as a reminder of the four ways in which God promised Moses he would redeem the children of Israel:

> I will bring you out from under the burdens of the Egyptians, and
> I will deliver you from their bondage,
> and I will redeem you with an outstretched arm, and with great judgments:
> and I will take you to Me for a people and be to you a God. (Exodus 6:6–7.)

Then his father washed his hands and passed everyone a kind of *hors d'oeuvres* of parsley or lettuce dipped in salt water. In front of him on a tray, there were three pieces of unleavened bread called Matzoth, the unleavened bread, a reminder that the children of Israel had to leave Egypt so hurriedly that there was no time for the dough to be leavened (Exodus 12:39). Two of the pieces were the double portions for Sabbaths and Holydays, and the third was known as 'the bread of affliction'. The three pieces also represented the priest, the Levite, and the children of Israel.

The middle piece of unleavened bread was broken in two by David's father. One piece was to be eaten during the meal, and the other, the 'aphikoman', from the Greek word for dessert, was to be eaten at the end of the meal.

With the Matzoth on the Seder table, there was also a baked egg, as a festival offering, and a shank bone, as a symbol of the Paschal lamb. David's father pointed to the unleavened bread, and everyone sitting round the table looked at it. Then he began reading the Haggadah:

> This is the bread of affliction that our ancestors ate in the land of Egypt. All who are hungry — let them come and eat: all who are needy — let them come and celebrate the Passover.

22

4. A Jewish family on Passover Eve.

Then, as the youngest member of the family, David had to ask the four famous questions.

The first question he asked was: 'Why is this night different from all other nights, for on all other nights we may eat leavened or unleavened bread, but on this night only unleavened.' This question was to show the importance of eating unleavened bread all through the Passover.

Then he asked the second question: 'On all other nights we may eat other kind of herbs, but on this night only bitter herbs,' which recalled the bitterness of slavery.

The third question was: 'On all other nights we need not dip our herbs even once, but on this night we do so twice.' Already the herbs had been dipped in salt water, but later the bitter herbs would be dipped in Haroseth, a mixture of apples, raisins, almonds, and cinnamon chopped together and mixed with wine to make a paste, as a reminder of the mortar used by the slaves to make magnificent buildings for their Egyptian masters.

The fourth question he asked was: 'On all other nights we eat either sitting or reclining, but on this night, we all recline.' This was a reminder of the way in which householders thousands of years ago reclined on cushions while they ate their meals, while the slaves had to eat so hurriedly that they sat on the floor.

Everyone joined in with David's father as he replied to the four questions:

We were Pharaoh's bondmen in Egypt; and the Lord brought us out of Egypt with a mighty hand. (Deuteronomy 6:21.)

Four examples of the way in which children should be told about the Passover story were given. For the son who was wise, the one who was wicked, the one who was rather slow, and the fourth was the one who didn't know what to ask or how to ask it. David hoped his father put him into the group of the wise son!

Israel, explained the Haggadah, had worshipped strange gods in the

5. Haggadah.

early days, and had then been brought close to the one true God. There had been Abraham, the 'Friend of God', Isaac his son, and Jacob and Esau his grandsons. Then Jacob and his children went down into Egypt, and their descendants became slaves until God rescued them. 'For the Holy One — determined the end of the bondage in order to fulfil that which he had said to Abraham our father, after his descendants had served as slaves in a strange land for four hundred years.' (Genesis 15:13, 14.)

And they all raised their cups of wine in thanksgiving to God, and sang a hymn:

> This faithfulness — has stood by our fathers and us — in every generation — the Holy One, Blessed be He, delivered us from the hands of the oppressors!

The story which followed of the way in which God delivered the Israelite slaves out of the hands of Pharaoh and the Egyptians, always seemed to David to be tremendously exciting.

There was the heartbreaking toil of the slaves day by day in the hot sun. Moses made his famous plea to Pharaoh: 'Let my people go!' (Exodus 5:1) but he would not let the Israelites go free. So God sent ten plagues.

When the Lord, with the tenth plague, smote all the first-born of the Egyptians at midnight, Pharaoh cried to Moses in the night: 'Rise up and get you forth from among my people . . . and go, serve the Lord, as ye have said.' (Exodus 12:29–31.)

There are three things which must be mentioned at Passover, and they are written in the Haggadah by Rabbi Gamaliel, a famous teacher. The first is the Passover itself. 'And ye shall say, "It is the sacrifice of the Lord's Passover, for that he *passed* over the houses of the children of Israel, when he smote the Egyptians . . ."' (Exodus 12:27.) The second is the un-leavened bread, because there was not time for the dough to become leavened as the children of Israel had to leave Egypt in such a hurry (Exodus 12:39). The third is 'this bitter herb which we eat', because 'they made their lives bitter with hard bondage, in mortar and in brick, and in all manner of service in the field — with rigour' (Exodus 1:14).

After that, David recited with all the others the very solemn words: 'In every single generation it is a man's duty to regard himself as if he had gone forth from Egypt' (Exodus 13:8). They all raised their glasses of wine and repeated words of praise and thanksgiving to God, 'Who performed for our fathers and for us all these wonders. He brought us forth from slavery to freedom . . . from darkness to great light. Let us sing before him, Hallelu-yah!'

And David knew that in Hebrew, Halleluyah meant the joyful words, 'Praise ye the Lord'.

Then there was more praise. From the Hallel, Hymns of Praise, Psalms 113 and 114, called the Egyptian Hallel, because Psalm 114 begins 'when Israel went forth out of Egypt . . .'

The first half of the Seder was almost ended. David's father blessed the second cup of wine, 'Blessed art Thou, O Lord our God, King of the Universe, Creator of the fruit of the vine,' and then everyone washed their hands, and portions of the upper and middle pieces of the unleavened bread were blessed and handed out. After another blessing, the bitter herb, the reminder of slavery, was dipped in the Haroseth, the mixture of apples, almonds, nuts and raisins. Then David's father broke the third piece of unleavened bread, and the real meal began with another blessing. Each person ate a piece of the unleavened bread like a sandwich with the bitter herb inside it, a custom begun by a great teacher called Rabbi Hillel, in the temple days, when people ate a portion of the Paschal Lamb, unleavened bread, and bitter herbs.

When the meal was over, David's father gave everyone a piece of the half of the middle Matzoth, which they had called 'aphikoman', for dessert. They all said grace, and the third cup of wine was drunk.

One cup of wine remained standing in the middle of the table. It was known as the cup of Elijah the prophet. It was there as a mark of welcome for Elijah, in the hope that he would soon come, because with him would come the age of the Messiah, when men all over the world would live in peace.

The second half of the Seder service included songs and tunes about Passover, and was all about God's redemption of the children of Israel. They drank the fourth cup of wine.

David joined with the others in singing lustily the final song 'Had Gadyah' which reminded him of a nursery rhyme. It began 'One only kid, one only kid, which my father bought for two zuzim (ancient coins); one only kid, one only kid . . .' and ended, 'then came the Most Holy blessed be he, and slew the angel of death who had slain the slaughterer, who had slaughtered the ox, which had drunk the water, which had extinguished the fire, which had burnt the staff, which had smitten the dog, which had bitten the cat, which had devoured the kid, which my father bought for two zuzim; one only kid, one only kid.'

The adults more than David understood that underneath the simple words was a very serious picture, because the song was really telling the history of Israel, of the dangers which had beset the Jewish people

26

6. Traditional Passover pilgrimage to Mount Zion in Jerusalem.

throughout the generations, and of how eventually God had destroyed the evil which threatened them.

The next morning, David, Jack and Jonathan each thought their Seder meal was the best, but David knew that the meal at his house was better than anyone else's anywhere, because when he went to bed that night, he had dreamed that Elijah visited their home and the whole world was at peace!

THE FESTIVAL OF THE GIVING OF THE TEN COMMANDMENTS

Seven weeks after Passover, everybody celebrated the Feast of Weeks — the season of the Giving of our Law. Before the festival the three boys read all about the time when God gave Moses the ten commandments on Mount Sinai.

The festival was also the Feast of the Harvest, described in Exodus 23:16, and the Day of the First Fruit Offering, described in Numbers 28:26. David, Jack and Jonathan and all the other pupils at their religion school helped to decorate the synagogue with sweet-smelling flowers and plants, and they learned that the plants and fruits, as well as looking lovely, had a deeper meaning.

The green plants and shrubs were like those that grow among the granite peaks of Mount Sinai, and the baskets of first fruits were like those brought in joyful processions by pilgrims to the temple to be presented to the priests from the Feast of Weeks to the Feast of Tabernacles (Exodus 23:19; Deuteronomy 26:2–4, 10). There was an old Rabbinic saying, too, that growing plants and trees were 'a memorial to the living joy of the Law'.

Most of the first night of the festival, David, his brother and his father and their friends and members of the synagogue, sat up reading passages from the Scriptures and other holy books. This preparation for the festivals was based on God's command that no one should touch the borders of Mount Sinai for three days before the tremendous event, when Moses was given the Ten Commandments.

David was tired in the morning, but he went with everyone else to the first service of the Feast of Weeks in the synagogue. A very important reading from the first five books of the Hebrew Scriptures, called the Sefer Torah or Scroll of the Law, was the story of the giving of the Ten Commandments. Everyone in the congregation stood while it was read out.

The original two stone tablets were kept in the Ark of the Covenant of the tabernacle, and later in the temple. In the synagogue where David and Jack and Jonathan were standing, there were two tablets placed above the Ark where the Scrolls of the Law were kept, on the eastern wall, facing Jerusalem. On the tablets were inscribed in Hebrew the opening words of the commandments:

1 I am the Lord thy God.
2 Thou shalt have no other gods before Me.
3 Thou shalt not take the name of the Lord thy God in vain.
4 Remember the Sabbath day, to keep it holy.
5 Honour thy father and thy mother.
6 Thou shalt not murder.
7 Thou shalt not commit adultery.
8 Thou shalt not steal.
9 Thou shalt not bear false witness against thy neighbour.
10 Thou shalt not covet.

All the three boys knew that there were two texts of the Ten Commandments, the original in Exodus 20:2–14, and the reminder given by Moses towards the end of his life, in Deuteronomy 5:6–18, when a new generation had grown up who were to enter the Promised Land. They knew that the Ten Commandments was a set of rules to help the Children of Israel to love God, and to love their neighbours (Deuteronomy 6:4–9 and Leviticus 19:18).

Then they read the book of Ruth because it describes the ancient harvest practice in Israel of inviting the poor and the stranger to glean in the fields, and because Ruth accepted the teachings of Judaism, which were foreign to her, with loving devotion. David had learned by heart her moving words: 'Thy people shall be my people, and thy God my God.'

King David, he reminded himself again proudly, was descended from Ruth, and it was during the Festival of Weeks that he died.

David invited Jack and Jonathan to share the festival meal at his home after the morning service in the synagogue. When they arrived home, they found the table laid, with two round loaves decorated with a ladder which, they were told, was a reminder of Moses going up to Mount Sinai, where he was given the Ten Commandments.

THE TEN DAYS OF REPENTANCE

(a) The New Year

The ten days between the Jewish New Year and the Day of Atonement, were called the 'Solemn Days' or the Ten Days of Repentance. When they arrived back from the synagogue on the eve of the New Year — Rosh Hashanah, or First of the Year — David always looked forward to the festive New Year meal, because there were apples dipped in honey to symbolize the hope that the *New Year would be a sweet and pleasant one.*

The two days of the New Year celebrations were kept as holy days recalling the act of creation. 'This is the day the world was called into existence,' was the way the festival Prayer Book put it. The New Year was the time when God 'caused all creation to stand in judgment.'

In the synagogue, the shofar, (Hebrew) ram's horn, was sounded during Morning Service. The quavering notes and long-drawn-out blasts of this biblical instrument were a stirring call to people that God, the King of the Universe, was giving them an opportunity to repent and return to him, to mend their ways and be forgiven.

The New Year was a hopeful time, pointing to a happier future, and a peaceful world, when 'all mankind shall form one single band to do his will with a perfect heart.'

(b) The Day of Atonement

Yom Kippur, the Day of Atonement, was the holiest day of the Jewish calendar. As it sounds, it means a time of trying to be 'at one' with God. All over the country Jewish people like David, Jack and Jonathan and their families, ate their last meal before the Eve of Yom Kippur, and then they fasted until the festival ended.

But it was not a time of gloom, or a 'black fast' as some people call it. It was a time, more than any other in the year, for feeling God's kindness and his love.

There was an air of excitement in the synagogue on the eve of the Day of Atonement, the beginning of the great religious event. The ark containing the Holy Scrolls and the reading desk had white covers, and the Rabbi and many of the worshippers wore white robes as a sign of purity and the

7. The Ram's Horn.

certainty of God's forgiveness.

The Cantor's singing of the opening prayer, Kol Nidre, or 'all vows', thrilled them because it was sung to magnificent music famous all over the world. David knew that it was asking God to forgive people who had failed to keep the promises they had made to him, through forgetfulness or mistake. The forgiveness only applied to vows made to God. Vows made between people could only be broken by agreement with the person himself.

The three boys stayed in the synagogue until nearly midnight, saying prayers with the adults. Some of the adults remained in the synagogue until the early hours of the morning.

The Day of Atonement was a day of continuous prayers. Like those of the New Year they included the theme of repentance (or return to God), and charity (or loving kindness to other people).

The Cantor wearing simple white robes, recited a prayer during the Morning Service, which was originally said by the High Priest on the Day of Atonement as he entered the Holy of Holies in the temple; and the three boys, like others in the synagogue, followed the old custom of prostrating themselves on the floor.

The Cantor solemnly confessed the sins of himself, and the people, as did the High Priest thousands of years ago in the ancient temple. Those present in the synagogue said, as had the people in the temple: 'Blessed be the Name whose Glorious Kingdom is for ever and ever'.

In the Morning Service, there was the reading from the holy prophets (Isaiah 57:14–58, 14) from which the following words are taken, 'Is not this the fast I have chosen . . . Is it not to deal thy bread to the hungry?'

In the afternoon service they read the book of Jonah. They thought about his grumbling and his obstinacy. They knew that the book had a very serious lesson to teach. It meant that God will forgive everyone who is really sorry for doing wrong.

The beautiful and moving service which ended the Day of Atonement began at sunset. It was called Neilah, because a long time ago the temple gates were closed at sunset, and Neilah meant the closing of the gates. Earlier they had prayed 'Inscribe us in the Book of Life'. But now as everyone remained standing, with the ark open throughout the service, the people prayed 'Seal us in the Book of Life.'

There were other prayers in beautiful Hebrew words meaning: 'O grant that we may enter thy gates, we pray Thee . . . Have mercy on us.' All through the day it had been the same message, right until the very end, God will forgive anyone who really repents. As the service ended the congrega-

32

tion repeated the age-old words of the Shema after the Cantor:

> Hear O Israel, the Lord our God, the Lord is one . . . Blessed be his Name, whose glorious Kingdom is forever and ever.

And the seven times repeated cry of the Israelites on Mount Carmel when the prophet Elijah challenged them to follow God:

> The Lord He is God! (1 Kings 18:18.)

Then came the sounding of the Ram's Horn. To David, Jack and Jonathan this was a challenge. As the Day of Atonement was the day of being at one with God, the sound of the horn blowing was a challenge to try to remain at one with God throughout the coming year.

THE FESTIVAL OF TABERNACLES

Five days after the Day of Atonement, the happy autumn Festival of the Tabernacles took place.

The Hebrew word for tabernacles was succah. 'You shall dwell in booths, (tabernacles), seven days,' David had read in the Book of Leviticus (23:42–43): 'so that your generation may know that I made the children of Israel to dwell in booths, when I brought them out of the land of Egypt.'

In memory of that time, when the Israelites had built frail little booths for themselves in the wilderness, David and Jack and Jonathan all helped their fathers to build tabernacles in their gardens. They made the roof from branches decorated with bright-coloured fruits and vegetables. Then they covered the walls with posters and drawings of the Holy Land. Inside the tabernacle they put special religious objects which they had made at school. Part of the roof was left open so that it was possible to see the heavens from inside the tabernacle.

The services of this festival were joyful. In the synagogue the boys held long palm branches called lulav in their right hands. With the palm there clustered flowering myrtles and willows. In their left hands they held a bright yellow citrus fruit (which looked like a lemon) the product of the Holy Land, called ethrog in Hebrew.

David stood next to his father and brother, and while the congregation

8. Buying palm branches for the Feast of Tabernacles.

recited the Hallel (Psalms 113–118, the Hebrew hymns of praise), he, the adults and all the other boys waved the ethrog and the palm branch in all directions as a sign that God is everywhere as God had commanded for the Feast of the Tabernacles:

> And ye shall take you on the first day, the fruit of the goodly trees, branches of palm trees, and boughs of thick trees, and willows of the brook, and ye shall rejoice before the Lord your God seven days. (Leviticus 23:40.)

Then David, Jack and Jonathan joined the other boys and adults marching round the synagogue in procession carrying the ethrog and lulav as the priests had once marched round the temple carrying palm branches and singing hymns of praise, and placing willows on the altar.

There are two Rabbinic explanations for the use of the four kinds of plants.

The first is that the tall palm branch stands for uprightness, the drooping willow for humility, the evergreen myrtle for constancy, and the citron (ethrog), with its fresh sweet smell, for affection, simplicity and gentleness.

34

9. Tabernacles in back gardens of homes in Jerusalem.

The second is that the palm symbolizes the spinal cord, the willow, the lips, the myrtle the eyes, and the citron the heart, because God must be served with all our being.

All the explanations, David found, stressed that the four different kinds of plants represented humanity: all sorts of people living together in true brotherhood and peace.

During the festival, the boys and their families really did 'dwell' in their tabernacles. They had their meals there, and on the first night of the festival they recited a prayer:

> May it be Thy will, O Lord, my God and God of my fathers, to let Thy Divine Presence abide among us. Spread over us the tabernacle of Thy Peace in recognition of the precept of the tabernacle which we are now fulfilling . . . O surround us with the pure and holy radiance of Thy Glory, that is spread over our heads as the eagle over the nest he stirreth up; and thence bid the stream of life flow in upon thy servant . . .
>
> Blessed be the Lord for ever . . . amen.

The seventh day of the festival was called Hoshaana Rabba, which means the Great Hoshaana. Many of the prayers began with the Hoshaana, the Prayer for Salvation: 'Save, we beseech Thee'.

Hoshaana Rabba, like the Day of Atonement, is one of the holiest days in the Jewish New Year, and all three boys had spent part of the previous night studying holy books with their fathers. Now they joined in seven processions, holding the ethrog and lulav and marching round the synagogue as the priests once marched round the temple.

On the eighth day, called the eighth day of Assembly, there was a special prayer for rain and a good harvest; from the days in ancient Israel when the people prayed for the food of life.

David didn't like rainy days, but their teacher made him think hard about the words of the prayer: it was a prayer for life and not for death; for abundance and not for famine. And David thought of the terrible droughts in some parts of the world, and the hunger and misery that they cause, and the prayer suddenly came to life.

SIMCHAT TORAH, THE HAPPIEST DAY IN THE JEWISH YEAR

Simchat Torah meant the rejoicing of the Torah; of the scriptures. It was the ninth and final day of the Festival of the Tabernacles, a time, full of joy. It was a time especially for the children. All of them, from the tiniest up to the bigger ones, like David, Jack and Jonathan, marched in procession with candles and banners singing hymns and following the bearers of the Sifre Torah, the sacred scrolls of the first five books of the Hebrew Scriptures.

The children were called to the reading of the Holy Bible, and the very young children were all gathered together and repeated the prayers which the adults said before the reading from the Torah.

David had always been taught that the reading from the Holy Scrolls never ceased, and this festival proved the truth of what he had learned.

10. Torah Bells.

11. Torah Crowns.

A member of the congregation, described as 'The Bridegroom of the Law' was called to the reading of the last section of the fifth book of the Hebrew Scriptures, Deuteronomy. Soon after, another member of the congregation, 'The Bridegroom of the first section of the Torah', was called for the reading of the first chapter of Genesis, the first book.

David thought back to what his teacher had told him, that the study and reading of God's words must continue throughout everyone's life.

Jack was thinking too, as he listened to the reading of the Holy Scriptures, of some words he had written in his religious school notes.

'Simchat Torah reminds Jews that their Torah is their priceless possession.'

Then they all went home, and because Simchat Torah is the happiest day of the Jewish Year, their parents and their friends gave them sweets and fruits and little presents.

CHANUKKAH, THE FESTIVAL OF DEDICATION AND OF LIGHTS

The mid-winter festival of Chanukkah is celebrated each year to remind Jews everywhere of the courage of a small band of men who fought for their faith against the pagan emperor, Antiochus of Syria, over two thousand years ago. Their story is told in the Book of Maccabees, and David copied down some words about them from the book:

'They were ready either to live or die nobly.'

Before the festival began, David read all about Judah the Maccabee, meaning Judah the Hammer, from the Hebrew word Makkebeth, who led the Israelites so bravely and cleverly that at last they 'hammered' the enemy. David copied out the name, *Maccabee*, and learned that the initials of the Hebrew word Maccabee made up the verse: 'Who is like unto Thee, O Lord, among the mighty ones?' (Exodus 15:11.)

Judah was the third son of an old priest, Mattathias, who started a revolt against the mighty pagan armies. The family lived in the small town of Modin, between Jerusalem and the sea. David and his friends read with horror of the terrible way in which the pagans treated the Jews, burning them and torturing them and throwing them over the city walls when they refused to deny their God — because when the emperor made a law enforcing pagan worship, they were ready to die rather than give up their faith.

38

12. Jewish children celebrate Chanukkah.

They read the terrible but moving story of Hannah and her seven heroic sons who were martyred one by one:

> But above all was the mother marvellous and worthy of honourable memory; for when she looked on seven sons perishing (to keep the faith) within the space of one day, she bore the sight with a good courage for the hopes she had set on the Lord . . . and last of all, after her sons, the mother died. (1 Maccabees.)

After three years' fighting, Judah, the Maccabee and his guerrilla warriors overcame the powerful armies of the emperor Antiochus. Judah ordered the cleansing of the temple, because debauchery and immorality had taken place inside it, and human sacrifices had been offered on the altar.

The menorah (lamps of the temple candelabrum), were lit, and although the pure oil needed to keep them burning was only enough for one night, it miraculously lasted for eight days until more oil arrived.

David watched his father light one candle in the menorah on the first night of Chanukkah. Each night after that, another candle was lit, until eight candles stood in the candelabrum. A shammash, the Hebrew for helper candle, was used to light the new candle each evening, and a blessing said: 'Blessed art Thou, O Lord our God . . . who . . . has commanded us to kindle the light of Chanukkah.'

Blessings were also said during the ceremony, thanking God for the miracles of that heroic time so long ago, and they all sang the hymn called Moaz Tzur: 'O Fortress, Rock of my salvation; unto Thee it is becoming to give praise.'

David, Jack and Jonathan went to Chanukkah parties and pageants, and all the children played games with a special four-sided top which they spun with their hands. On its sides were inscribed the four opening letters of the Hebrew words meaning 'A great miracle happened here.'

Chanukkah to David was a great festival of light and gaiety, with its candles and hymns and stories of heroes and heroines. Sometimes he wished he could join in the Chanukkah festivals in Israel today, when lighted torches are carried all the way from Modin, where the revolt began, to Mount Zion in Jerusalem.

THE FESTIVAL OF PURIM

David and his friends had made a special study of the Festival of Purim, because they were putting on a play about it for the parents and teachers and all the other pupils at their religion school.

David was to play Mordecai, one of the lead parts, and he had read in the Book of Esther. all about the history of the festival.

Mordecai was a Jew in Persia over two thousand, four hundred years ago, who refused to bow down before Haman, the Chief Minister to the Persian King, Ahaseurus. Mordecai said he would bow down to no one but God, and Haman was so angry that he not only vowed to kill Mordecai, but to kill all the Jews.

Purim is the Hebrew word for lots. Haman cast lots to decide which month would be lucky for him to carry out his plot against the Jews, and the lots fell to the 13th day of the month of Adar, in the spring.

When the day came, Haman went to King Ahaseurus and told him lies about the Jews. Then he offered the King a fortune for his consent to have them put to death.

But Mordecai heard about the plot, and he told his beautiful cousin,

40

13. Scroll of Esther.

Esther, who was Ahaseurus' Queen, that she and all the Jewish people were thus threatened.

Although Esther was Queen, she knew that if she went before the King when he had not summoned her, her life would be in danger. Before she risked her life, she asked Mordecai to gather all the Jews and join her in fasting for three days first, so that God would have mercy and help her.

'Then,' she said, 'I will go unto the King. And if I perish, I perish.'

After the three days' fasting, Esther dressed herself in her most beautiful clothes, and went to the innermost court of the palace, where King Ahaseurus was sitting on his throne. Esther came near to the King. And he asked her what was her wish; 'Even to half of the kingdom shall it be given to you', so strong was his affection for her. Esther asked if he and Haman would come to a banquet, and the King agreed.

Haman was delighted because it was a great honour to be asked to accompany Ahaseurus to a banquet given by the Queen. He had a massive gallows erected, and planned to hang Mordecai from it first, so that he could really enjoy the feast.

14. The Feast of Purim Carnival in Israel.

On that night the King could not sleep. He had the book of events read to him and heard a report how Mordecai had saved his life by uncovering a plot to kill him. The King was so grateful that he ordered Haman to have Mordecai dressed in royal robes and to ride through the city and Haman proclaimed that Mordecai was being honoured by the King for his loyalty. Later at the second banquet, Esther accused Haman of plotting to destroy all the Jews in the Persian Empire, and the King had him hanged from the gallows he had built for Mordecai.

David was not the only one with an important part in the play. Jack was to be the King, Ahaseurus, and Hadassah, David's cousin, was taking the title role as Esther. They kept the 13th of the month of Adar as a fast, in memory of Esther's fast, and on the 14th Adar and on the evening before the 13th Adar, in the synagogue, Esther's story was read out. Then on the evening of the festival, the children gave their play, and it was a great success.

Afterwards they held a big Purim party, and David, Jack, Jonathan and Hadassah ate delicious three-cornered pastries called Hamantaschen, which was full of poppy seeds. Then David read a letter to them all from his Israeli pen friend, Isaac, about the Festival of Purim in Israel, where the story of Esther is retold in carnivals in the streets of Tel Aviv and in all the big cities.

DAVID'S BAR-MITZVAH

David's Bar-Mitzvah, his religious coming-of-age, took place on the Sabbath of his thirteenth birthday on 20th October 1973. It meant that he would become a 'Son of the Commandment', a responsible person and it was a very important day in his life — a religious milestone.

The ceremony was to take place in the synagogue. The Greek word is *synagoge*, but the Hebrew was Beth Knesset or House of Assembly of prayer and study. David was very excited. He had spent a long time studying and preparing for this day, and he was thrilled because his teachers said he had done well. He and Jack and Jonathan arrived together, with their families, for shacharit, the morning service. David wore his tallith — his praying shawl — with its fringes reminding him to carry out God's commandments, and an embroidered silk cap. He felt a little nervous at first.

When shacharit ended, the congregation stood up and the Cantor went to the Ark containing the scrolls of the first five books of the Hebrew Bible. The Ark was opened, and a prayer said: 'For out of Zion shall go forth the Law, and the Word of the Lord from Jerusalem . . .'

Then the Cantor took the scrolls and said 'Blessed be he who in his Holiness gave the Law to his People, Israel.'

After the prayer were the blessings. Everyone joined in it: 'Hear, O Israel, the Lord our God, the Lord is One . . .'

David's great moment had come.

He was called by his Hebrew name, 'David son of Jacob', and he had to mount the bima or platform, and stand at the reading desk on which the Holy Scroll had been placed.

Members of the congregation including his father and brother were called up in turn, and David chanted seven portions from Genesis, the first book of the Hebrew Bible. Hebrew is read from right to left instead of left to right, as is English. David chanted according to an early system of musical notation — from the first six chapters of Genesis, which contained the story of the creation and what it meant in the religion of Judaism.

'This is the book of the generation of Adam,' David chanted from Chapter 5. He knew that Adam meant man, and that one of the greatest teachings in the Torah was the unity of the human race and the belief in the brotherhood of man.

As his last reading from the scroll, David chanted verses from the Maftir, the sixth chapter of Genesis. Then the scroll was spread out and held up by a member of the congregation so that everyone could see it. Then the congregation sat down.

Another worshipper came and rolled up the scroll, and tied a sash round it. An embroidered mantle was laid on top of the scroll, covered by a breastplate as a reminder of the one once worn by the High Priest, with twelve precious stones, representing the twelve tribes of Israel. On the breastplate was placed a pointer used when the scroll was being read, and a Torah crown over the ends of the rollers of the scroll.

Lastly, David chanted the Haftorah, the conclusion, a lesson from the prophet Isaiah (42:5–43:10). It showed very clearly the link between the teaching of Isaiah and the first chapters of Genesis which David had just read. It began:

> Thus saith God, the Lord; He that created the heavens, and stretched them forth; He that spread abroad the earth and that which comes out of it. He that gives breath to the people upon it, and spirit to them that walk therein.

In the sermon that followed, the Rabbi of the synagogue told David that he was now a full member of his religious community, and he said how much they looked forward to seeing him take part in their worship and service. He told David that as a young Jew, he now had a good foundation of the teachings of Judaism, and that he must continue with his studies as he grew up to manhood.

Then he blessed David with the benediction David loved so much:

> The Lord bless thee and keep thee:
> The Lord make his face to shine upon thee; and be gracious unto thee:
> The Lord lift up his countenance upon thee, and give thee peace.

David's parents gave a party to celebrate his Bar-Mitzvah. During it, he gave a talk which he had spent a long time preparing. It was about the creation, about God, who made the world, and about man whom God made to live according to his laws. Then he thanked his parents and teachers for helping him to understand a little about his faith, and friends and relations for their presents.

The day after David's Bar-Mitzvah was a Sunday, and in the morning,

44

15. Bar-Mitzvah boys from Youth Aliyah Children's Village at the Western Wall, Jerusalem.

he went to the synagogue. Now that he was of age, he was included in the quorum, the number of ten people needed for a congregation for public worship.

First he put on the tallith (Hebrew for praying shawl), and said a blessing: 'Blessed art Thou, O Lord our God, King of the Universe, who has commanded us to wrap ourselves in the fringed garment.'

Jack and Jonathan watched closely as he put on the tephillin, because in a few months' time they, too, were to be Bar-Mitzvah. They knew it was connected with the Hebrew word *tephillah*, which meant prayer.

The wearing of the tephillin (which is a plural noun) was based on four passages in the Hebrew Bible, Deuteronomy 6:4–9 and 11:13–21, and Exodus 13:1–10 and 13:11–16. The passages were written on parchment and placed in small black leather boxes.

As he placed one tephillah (which is a singular noun) on his left arm above the elbow, facing in to his heart, David twisted the strap seven times round his arm and repeated the ancient commandment to wear the tephillin. He repeated a similar commandment as he placed the other tephillah over the middle of his forehead, with the knots of the straps placed on the back of his head, at the middle of the neck and two straps hanging down either side in front of his shoulders.

16. Torah Breast Plate.

To wear the tephillin was like wearing a bridal garland. It was a sign of the love and devotion which exists between the children of Israel and God. The tephillah strapped on David's head was a sign that he must worship God with all his mind, and the tephillah on his arm, facing his heart, was a sign that he was to worship God with all his heart. As he wound the straps three times round his middle finger, David recited beautiful words taken from the prophet Hosea (2:21—22):

> And I will betroth thee unto Me for ever . . .
> I will betroth thee unto Me, in righteousness . . . justice, lovingkindness and compassion.
> And I will betroth thee unto Me in faithfulness; and thou shalt know the Lord.

SARAH'S WEDDING

There was an air of excitement in David's house as Sarah's wedding day approached. She was to marry Abraham. The family had known him for a long time, and they liked him. David thought of Abraham as a good friend, and looked forward to having him as a brother-in-law.

Jack and Jonathan were invited to the service in the synagogue on Sarah's wedding day. Beforehand, all three boys had made a study of the Jewish marriage ceremony. In Hebrew it was called Kiddushin. In Judaism, marriage is a very holy thing. It is called the Covenant of God, and Kiddushin means 'to be holy'.

Abraham, the bridegroom, stood with his father beneath a velvet chuppa or canopy. There were flowers round the four poles of the canopy, and embroidered on the overhanging velvet edges were the Hebrew words:

'The voice of joy and gladness, the voice of the bridegroom and of the bride.'

In a hushed silence, everyone watched Sarah walk slowly forward with her father. She wore a white wedding dress and a long white veil. Behind her walked her mother and Abraham's mother, the bridesmaids and the best man. The Cantor started to sing a welcome:

'Blessed be the one who comes in the name of the Lord, we bless you out of the House of the Lord!'

Then as he chanted other blessings, Sarah went to stand beside

Abraham under the canopy, facing the Ark containing the Holy Scrolls of the Torah.

With their parents standing on either side of them and their bridesmaids and best man behind them, Sarah and Abraham listened to the Rabbi as he talked to them about marriage. The canopy, he said, was a symbol of their future home, and it would be their duty to keep their home holy.

When he finished speaking, he chanted the 'Blessing of Betrothal' over a goblet of wine, and the bride and groom both took a sip from it.

Abraham placed a plain golden ring on the forefinger of Sarah's right hand and said: 'Behold, thou art consecrated unto me by this ring according to the Law of Moses and of Israel.' Then the Rabbi read a passage from the Ketubah, the marriage contract which Abraham had signed. In it, he promised to be a true husband, to honour and cherish Sarah, to work for her, protect her and support her.

When the reading had ended, the Cantor chanted seven blessings in praise of God for his acts of creation, including creating man in his own image. In the blessings were the words 'The Voice of joy and gladness, the voice of the bridegroom and of the bride,' and David's eyes wandered back to the same words embroidered so intricately on the velvet canopy.

The blessings were chanted over a goblet of wine, and afterwards, Sarah and Abraham again sipped the blessed wine. Then Abraham broke a glass under his foot, and the congregation cried out 'Mazzal Tov!' (Good Luck! – Congratulations!) Abraham had explained this act to David earlier when they were talking about the marriage ceremony. It was a reminder to the newly married couple not to be so joyful that they forgot their responsibilities, and a reminder of the destruction of the temple, which Jewish people would never forget.

Abraham and Sarah were now man and wife; and the service ended with those words which by now David knew so well:

The Lord bless thee and keep thee:
The Lord make his face to shine upon thee; and be gracious unto thee:
The Lord lift up his countenance upon thee, and give thee peace.

The wedding banquet after the service was a very happy occasion. The Cantor and the Rabbi joined the two families and all their friends, and the Cantor began the feast by chanting a blessing over the bread. There were speeches made in honour of the bride and the bridegroom, and Abraham had to make a speech in reply.

After the meal, the Cantor chanted grace and repeated the seven

17. Marriage Contract.

18. Ceremonial Marriage Rings.

blessings of the marriage service again: 'The Voice of joy and gladness, the voice of the bridegroom and of the bride . . .'

David joined heartily in the singing of Hebrew songs played by an orchestra, especially a very jolly one called 'Hava Nagila' — Come, sing and be happy!

SYMBOLS OF JUDAISM

There are two chief symbols of Judaism. One is the Menorah, and the other is the Shield of David. Jonathan decided to study the origins of these two important symbols.

The Menorah is the oldest Jewish symbol. It was a seven-branched candelabrum made of fine gold and ornamented with cups and almond flowers. It was made by a master-craftsman called Bezalel and placed in the Sanctuary of the Tabernacles where it was always kept alight, its lamps filled daily with oil (Exodus 25:31—40; 27:20—21).

Later, the menorah was placed in the temple. Today every synagogue has a continually burning light — the *Ner Tamid* in front of the Ark containing the Scrolls of the Torah.

When Jonathan visited the Jewish Museum with David and Jack and other boys at their religion school, he saw beautiful examples of the menorah, some very old indeed. He sketched some of them in his school book, and he wrote an essay on the menorah, explaining that it had become an early symbol of Judaism. It was now the symbol of the State of Israel, where a giant bronze menorah with panels of biblical scenes stands outside the Parliament of Israel — the Knesset in Jerusalem.

The Shield or Star of David, is two interlaced triangles. It was found on tombstones and old Jewish buildings in the Holy Land and other countries, and began to be used as a Jewish symbol about seven hundred years ago. Jonathan found that it was embroidered on many of the synagogue coverings and vestments, and that many Jewish organizations used it too.

It was difficult for him to find out how the symbol began. There were three possible answers. One was that the star represented a bow which King David used as a shield. Another, that it was really the capital letter D for David, because the old form of D, the Hebrew Daleth, was made in the shape of a triangle, rather like the Greek letter Delta. The third explanation was that the six-sided figure in the middle of the triangles represented the Holy Sabbath, and the six corners were the six working days.